037 698

837875

KU-419-406

DISCARD

B.C.H.E. — LIBRARY

00046447

My Word

C. A. SIMS

Designed by T.H.B.Russell MSIA

Illustrated by Rex Ripley

Contents

both ear
cardigan jumper
clothes mine
curly pair
difference same
each straight

head
hair
forehead
eyes
nose
mouth
chin
neck

cap

shirt
pullover
sleeve

hat

sweater

arms

dress

trousers
shorts

hands

legs

stockings

socks

feet

sandals

shoes

2 Mummy

hair
long short
blonde dark

cares

blouse

tall pretty
smart

works

takes

apron

skirt

cooks

always   her   love
dress   hug   woman
good   hurt

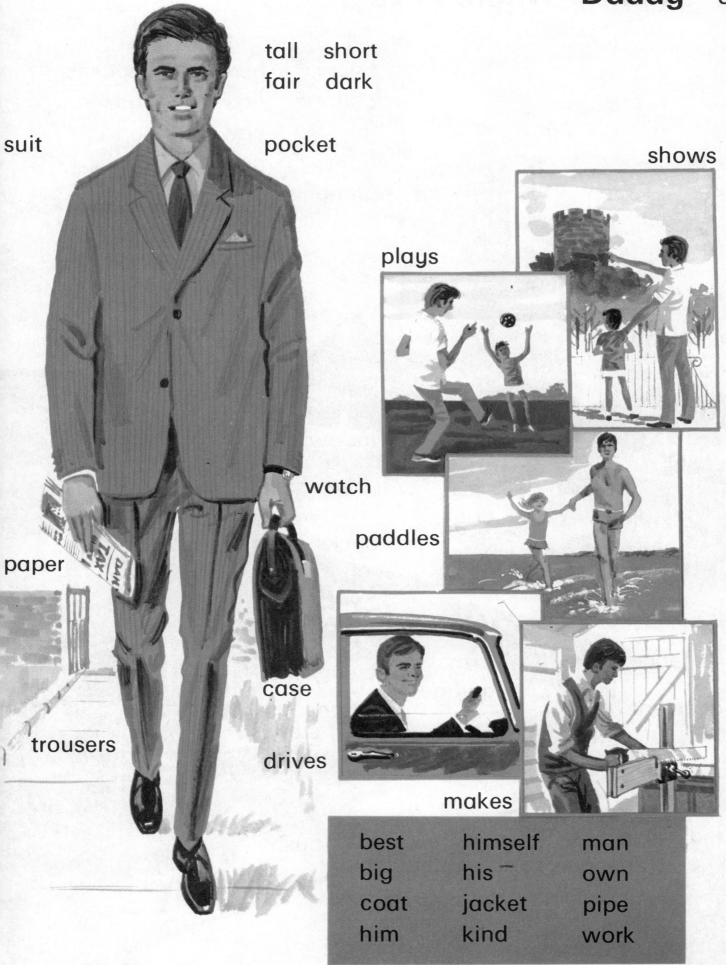

tall short
fair dark

suit

pocket

shows

plays

watch

paddles

paper

case

drives

trousers

makes

best	himself	man
big	his	own
coat	jacket	pipe
him	kind	work

4 Home – where I live

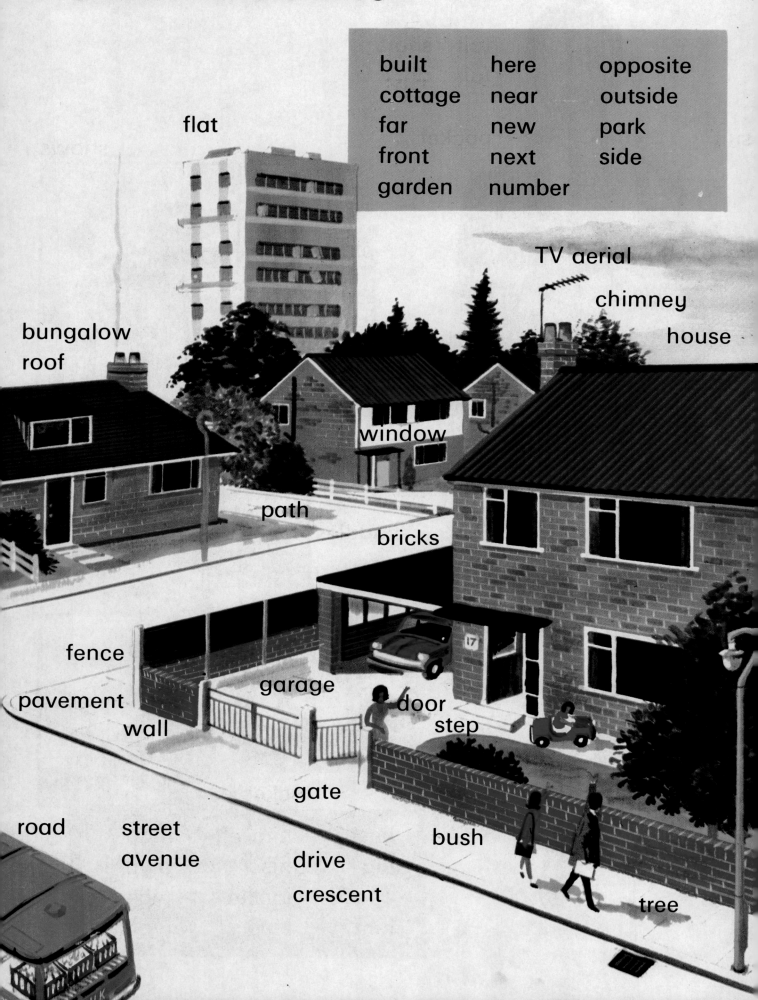

built   here   opposite
cottage   near   outside
far   new   park
front   next   side
garden   number

flat

TV aerial

chimney

house

bungalow
roof

window

path

bricks

fence

pavement

garage

door

wall

step

gate

road   street

bush

avenue   drive

crescent

tree

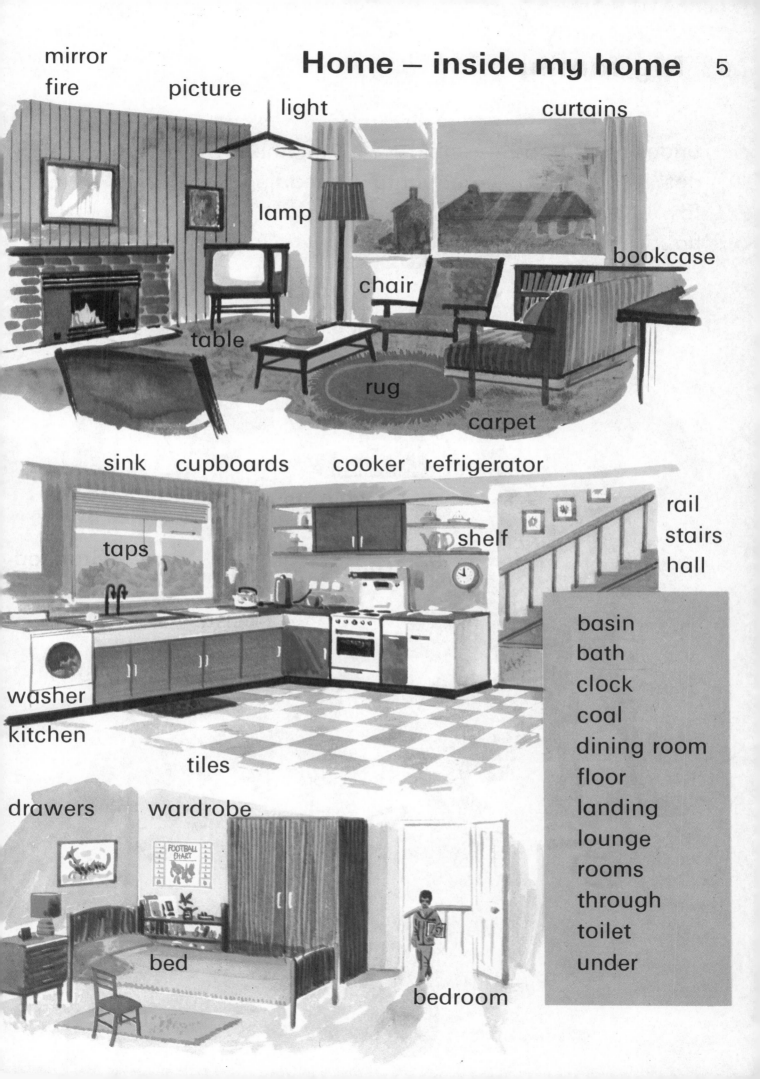

mirror

fire

picture

Home – inside my home 5

light

curtains

lamp

chair

bookcase

table

rug

carpet

sink   cupboards   cooker   refrigerator

rail

stairs

hall

taps

shelf

washer

kitchen

tiles

drawers   wardrobe

FOOTBALL CHART

bed

bedroom

basin
bath
clock
coal
dining room
floor
landing
lounge
rooms
through
toilet
under

6 My family

bridesmaid hope mind together
cot knit naughty wedding
favourite marry people
happy meet photograph

Mummy Uncle

Auntie

cousins

Daddy

Grandad
Grandma

sister

baby

brother

food   drink

born	ginger	mess	stroke
feed	give	mice	tabby
finger	keep	nip	wagging
fluffy	kept	open	
gently	little	soft	

bird   budgerigar

pony   stable

basket   kittens

cage

puppy

cat

mouse

hamster

dog

kennel

hutch

rabbit   guinea pig

8 Dressing up

nurse
umbrella red cross
bowler
soldier
helmet
crown
queen
uniform
sword
belt
robes
stetson
hat
feather
head-dress
scarf
bow and arrow
spaceman

docto
coc
ba
su
boot

act   feel   prince   wear
clothes   princess
dress   odd   put   smiling

black cat

cloak

witch

wand

star

demon

wizard

fairy

ring

coach

wishing well

glass slipper

bad	fright	secret
broke	giant	stone
dragon	king	treasure
dwarf	might	tricks
first	number	vanish

lamp

bottle	end	only
build	jumping jack	shining
crackers	lit	soon
down	month	start

break half minute show
every hour music tonight
favourite late week
film listen puppet

animals

set
screen
picture

cartoon

switch

Western

sit watch
look

crime

news

programme

12 At the zoo

elephant giraffe

animals fierce keeper tame
been fox many took
began free met wild
cub grizzly monkey

chimpanzee

gorilla

zebra

cage

tiger

lion

wolf

crowd

people

bears

peacock

hippopotamus

herons

penguins

seals

turtle

pelican

streamer

balloons

fairy

tree

lights

star

Father
Christmas

Santa
Claus

chimney

snow

singing
carols

card

presents

sack

angel	fun	kings	real
Bethlehem	happy	left	robin
chocolate	holly	please	shepherds
crib	Jesus	poor	won

nativity

play

14 My school

back   clay   learn   story
bell   colour   page   sum
bowl   desk   playground   tell
caretaker   how   pray   write

Friday
litre
My Wor
Topic

board
class
lesson
teacher

wendy
house

maths   water

sand

draw
paint

satchel

build
bricks

brushe

books
read   sit

ANIMALS
OF THE
WORLD

pencils
crayons

chair

stop

hand

helmet

The policeman 15

horse mounted

arm radio

uniform

crowd
wave

control

search
handler

panda
aerial

traffic

lead dog

across
along
ask
driver
job
lost
measure
would

patrol

road

accident hurt crash ambulance help

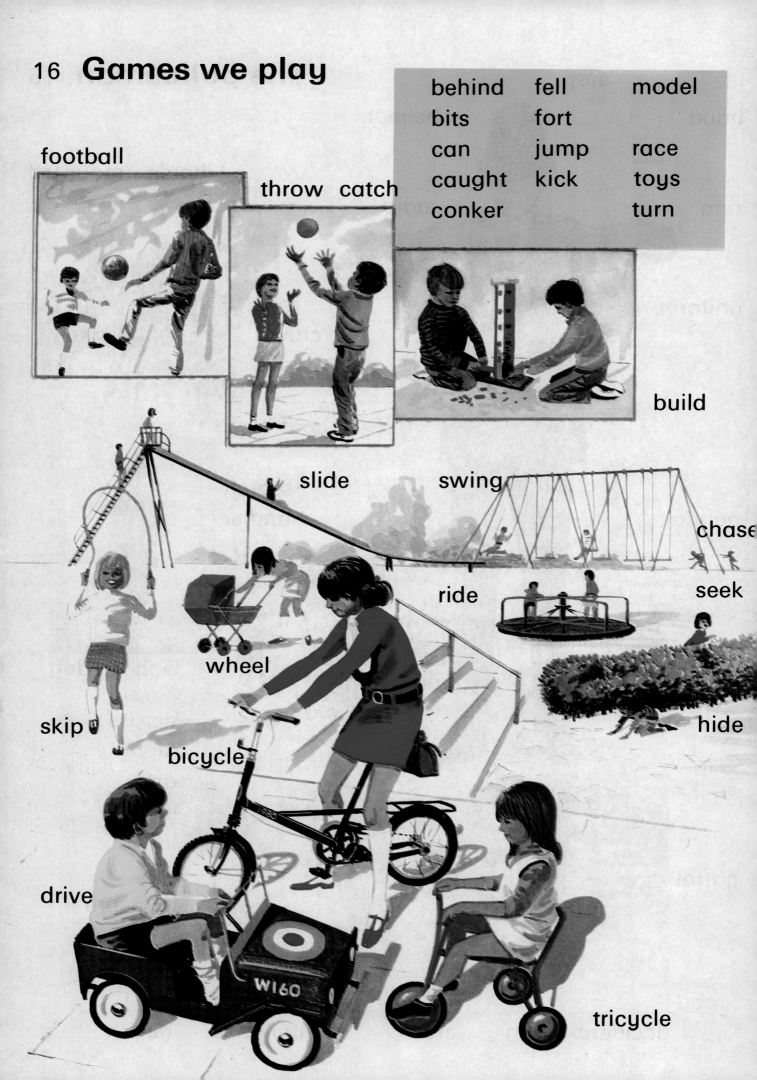

football

throw catch

behind	fell	model
bits	fort	
can	jump	race
caught	kick	toys
conker		turn

build

slide   swing

chase

ride   seek

wheel

skip

bicycle

hide

drive

tricycle

lions

juggler

trapeze

band

crowd

stilts

caravan   tent

elephants

rider

seal

acrobats

dogs

clowns

horse

costume

ring

acts	drop	finished	high	tail	tomorrow
animals	end	great	laugh	ticket	top
circles	fall	hard	over	today	tower

18 Mealtime

dinner

soup pudding

potatoes
vegetables
meat

tea bread water

tarts

jam

cakes butter

breakfast

cornflakes
milk coffee

cocoa

egg

toast fruit

best	cup	full	pancake
biscuit	cut	hungry	piece
buns	eat	jelly	sweet
chips	enough	lump	

ice cream

Harvest Festival 19

book
bring
chosen
classes

floor
gifts
hymn

morning
pray
quiet
read

sing
sit
stand
story

thanks
tune

hall

numbers

grown-ups
Headmistress
piano
teacher
corn
table
stage
ivy
berries
fruit
children
cabbage
groceries
tea
carrots
cheese
eggs
potatoes
vegetables
tomatoes

20 Shopping

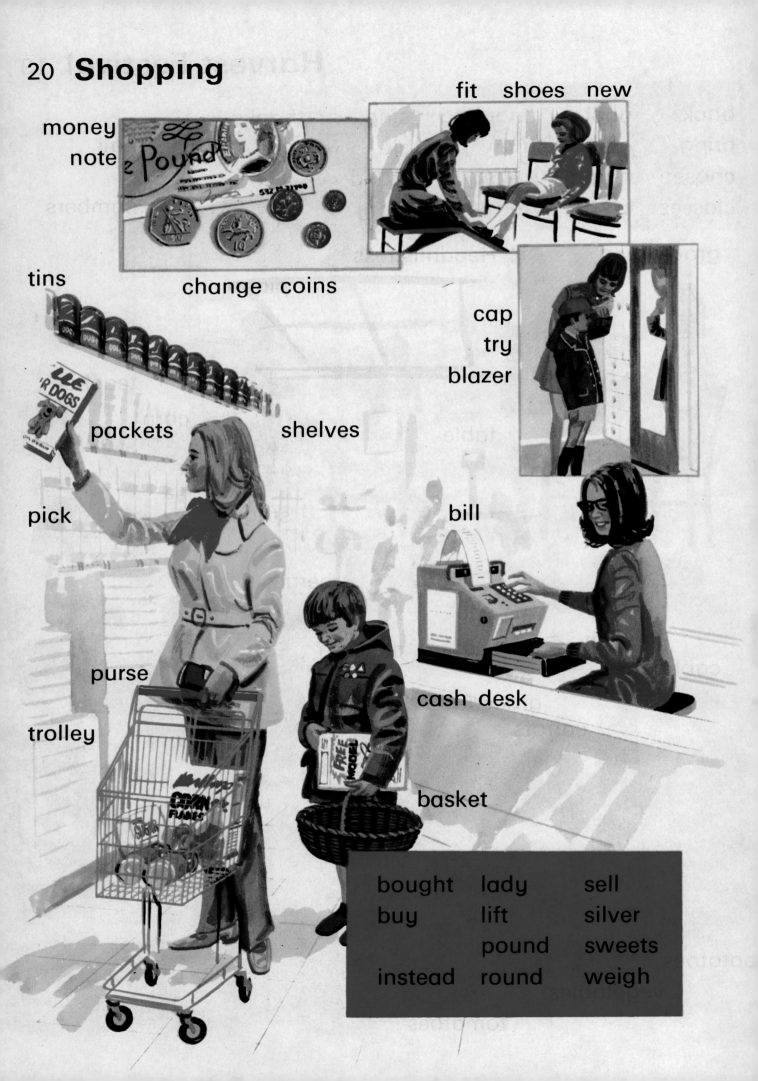

money
note
fit   shoes   new
tins
change   coins
cap
try
blazer
packets   shelves
pick
bill
purse
cash desk
trolley
basket

bought   lady   sell
buy   lift   silver
          pound   sweets
instead   round   weigh

On the farm 21

animals country land quack
bull field mud woods
corn harvest plough wool

shed hay dairy stable

barn horse

tractor

cow

calf yard

goose duck

pond

pig sheep

lamb

piglets baby cock

hen

chicks straw fork

bale

blue sky

planes

kite

balloon

glider

helicopter

wasp

birds

clouds

bee

fly

butterfly

rocket

bat

moth

float   seeds
hill   white
jet   wind

time   six o'clock

goodbye

after	dance	invitation	sing
come	every	leave	tea
could	gave	letter	write
cut	hello	ready	yes

6 Hill Woodley

Dear Michael

Thank you for a very nice time at your party.

Katie

note

friends

welcome

balloon

hats

laugh

games

cards

presents

candles

cake

drink

table

cloth

sandwiches

sign

ranch

brave
change
dust
fight
get
hit
kill
shoot
stony

wigwam
skins

sheriff

chief

head-dress

feather

stetson

how

shirt

scarf
badge
waistcoat

rope

gun

chaps

spurs

fire

blanket
tomahawk

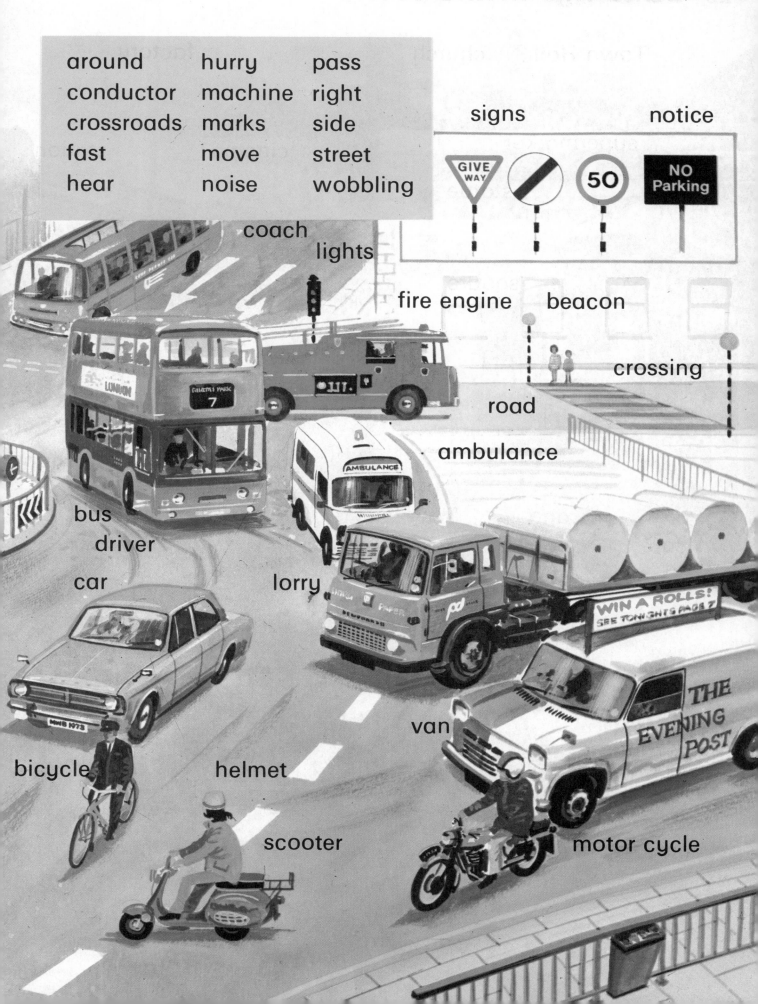

around   hurry   pass
conductor   machine   right
crossroads   marks   side
fast   move   street
hear   noise   wobbling

signs   notice

GIVE WAY   50   NO Parking

coach
lights
fire engine   beacon
crossing
road
ambulance
bus
driver
car   lorry
WIN A ROLLS! SEE TONIGHTS PAGE 7
van   THE EVENING POST
bicycle   helmet
scooter   motor cycle

Buildings in the town

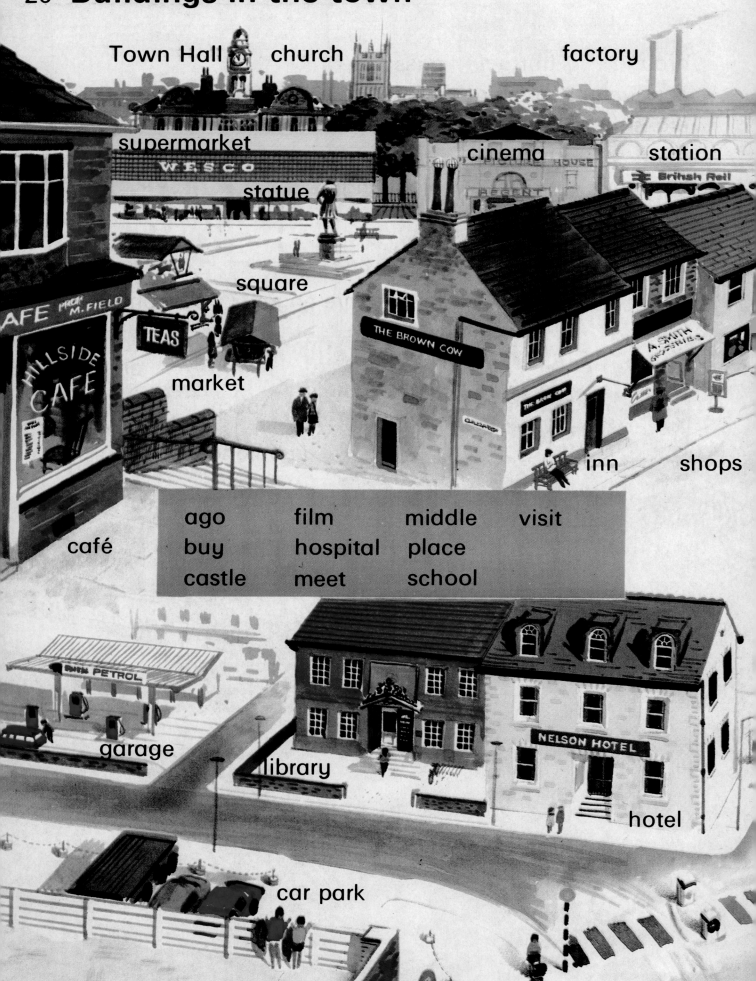

Town Hall church factory

supermarket cinema station

statue

square

market

café

inn shops

ago film middle visit
buy hospital place
castle meet school

garage library hotel

car park

bulb   garden   nature   plant
bunch   leaf   number pretty
collect   leaves   pick   under

snowdrop

crocus

daffodil

tulip

wallflower

aster

rose

poppy
forget-me-not
daisy

pink

vase

pansy

28 Helping Mummy

stairs   clean

carry

cover   house   something
dirt   polish   yesterday
dust   pram

bed   path   sweep   brush

make

dry

pegs   clothes   hang out

sheets

lay table

place

wet   sink

wash up

drain

hot   cooker

cook

door

ready

bake

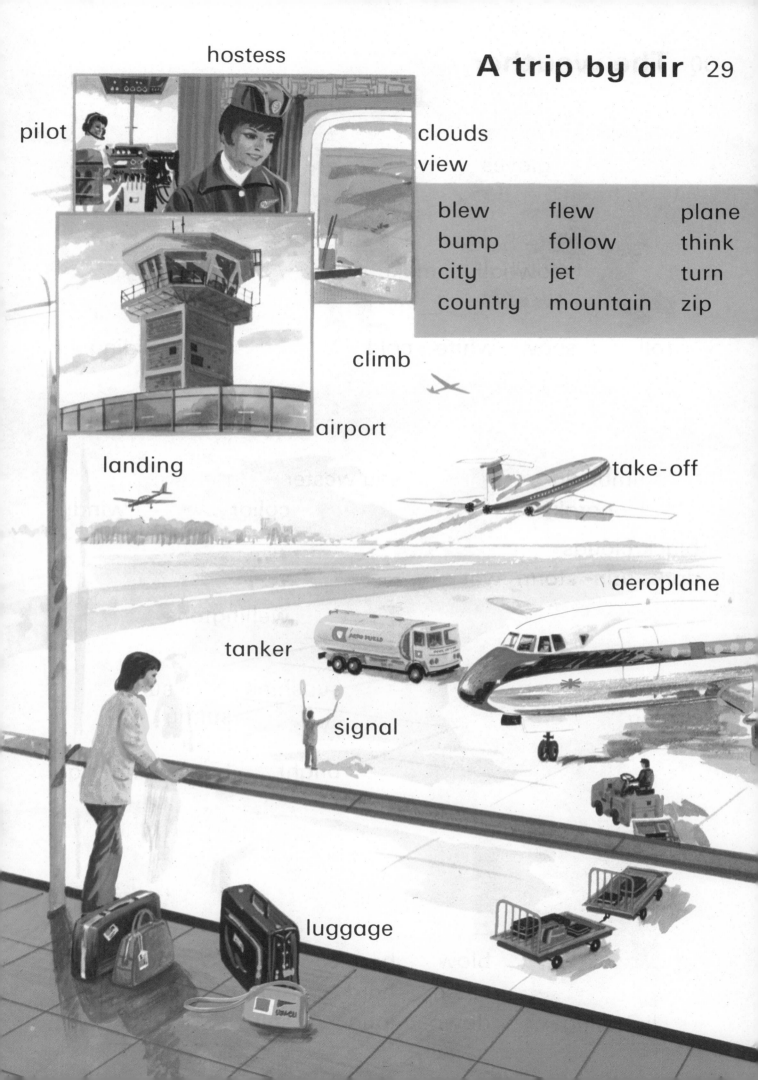

hostess

pilot

clouds
view

blew	flew	plane
bump	follow	think
city	jet	turn
country	mountain	zip

climb

airport

landing

take-off

aeroplane

tanker

signal

luggage

snowman

gloves

scarf
duffel coat

snowball   make   sledging

roll   snow   white   cold   sliding

umbrella   sou'wester
anorak   collar   windy

black clouds
dark   rain   storm   wet

wellingtons

thick   sunshine   sun
fog   sunny

bright   hot   warm   tan

lightning

blow	happen	sleet	thunder
crash	hard	softly	wind
down	loud	still	

starling

sparrow

winter

flock

kingfisher

beak

river

rush

sing

eagle

talons

robin   red

bill   hole   tiny
eggs   house   vulture
feathers   nest   wings

cuckoo

tail

seagull

wren

claws

woodpecker

blackbird

swan

webbed   white

away
costume
donkey
expect
fill

find
new
stay
swim

very
visit
waiting
water

sun hat

glasses

ring

T shirt

shorts

flag

castle

rock

trunk

sand

spade

goggles

bucket

towel

flippers

shells

seaweed   pool

net   jar   starfish   crab

battle   miss
beach   must
calm   rough
drown   sails
jacket   trip

warship

captain   liner   steamer   lighthouse

sailor   flags   rocks

OUR MASTER

boat   motor-boat   yacht

lifebelt   deck

waves

dinghy   oar

canoe
paddles

34 Helping Daddy

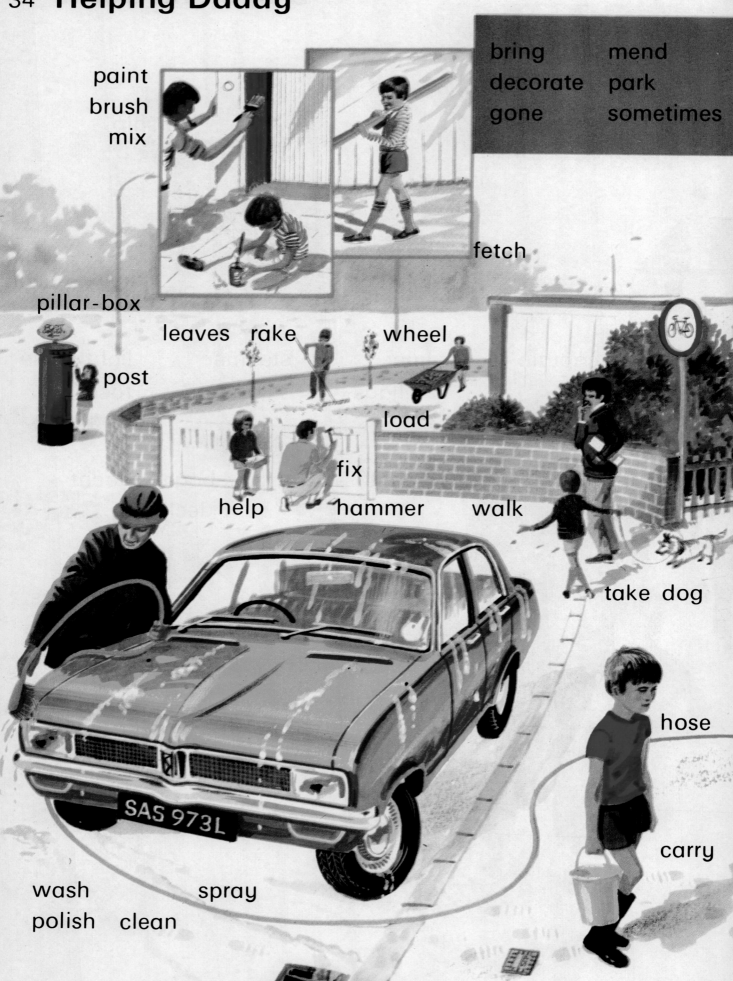

paint
brush
mix

bring   mend
decorate   park
gone   sometimes

fetch

pillar-box

leaves   rake   wheel

post

load

fix

help   hammer   walk

take dog

hose

carry

wash   spray
polish   clean

SAS 973L

Looking at railways 35

rack

luggage

corridor

seat

crane	men	push
diesel	points	stop
electric	pull	wait

passengers

box signal bridge

truck van

guard

station

taxi

posters

carriage

engine

office

nam

porter

case

track lines

platform

lamp

orchard

ate	nice	sour
green	pips	stones
juicy	ripe	sweet
leaves	skin	taste

currants
blackberries

jam

raspberries
damsons

cherries

fruit salad

bananas
18p kg

oranges
3 FOR 7p

apples
30p kg

pears
31p kg

plums
45p kg

peaches
4p EACH

grapefruit
10p EACH

lemons
8 PF OR 2

gooseberries
15p kg

grapes
20p ½ kg

strawberries
10p PER PUNNET

sleep   doll

afternoon	clean	temperature
better	cry	until
call	dentist	wake
came	morning	

telephone

doctor

ill   hot   feel

keep
thermometer

jigsaw
radio   read
listen   comic

straw

fruit

drink

glass jug

38 The postman

address   collect   knock
also   early   name
any   find   write

letter
stamp

postcard

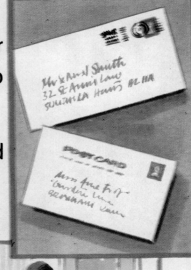

cards   on show

take

cap
badge

hurry

letter-box

push   bag

carry
package

parcel

empty   open

van

pillar-box

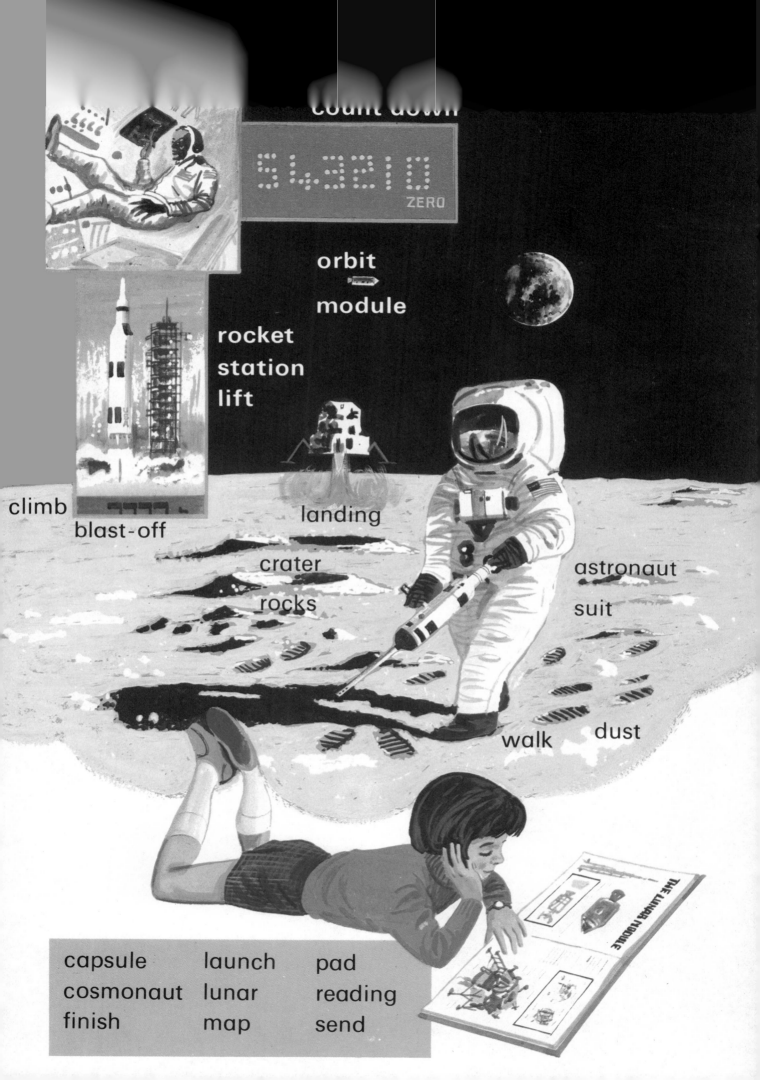

count down

5 4 3 2 1 0
ZERO

orbit

module

rocket
station
lift

climb

blast-off

landing

crater

rocks

astronaut

suit

walk

dust

capsule   launch   pad
cosmonaut lunar   reading
finish   map   send

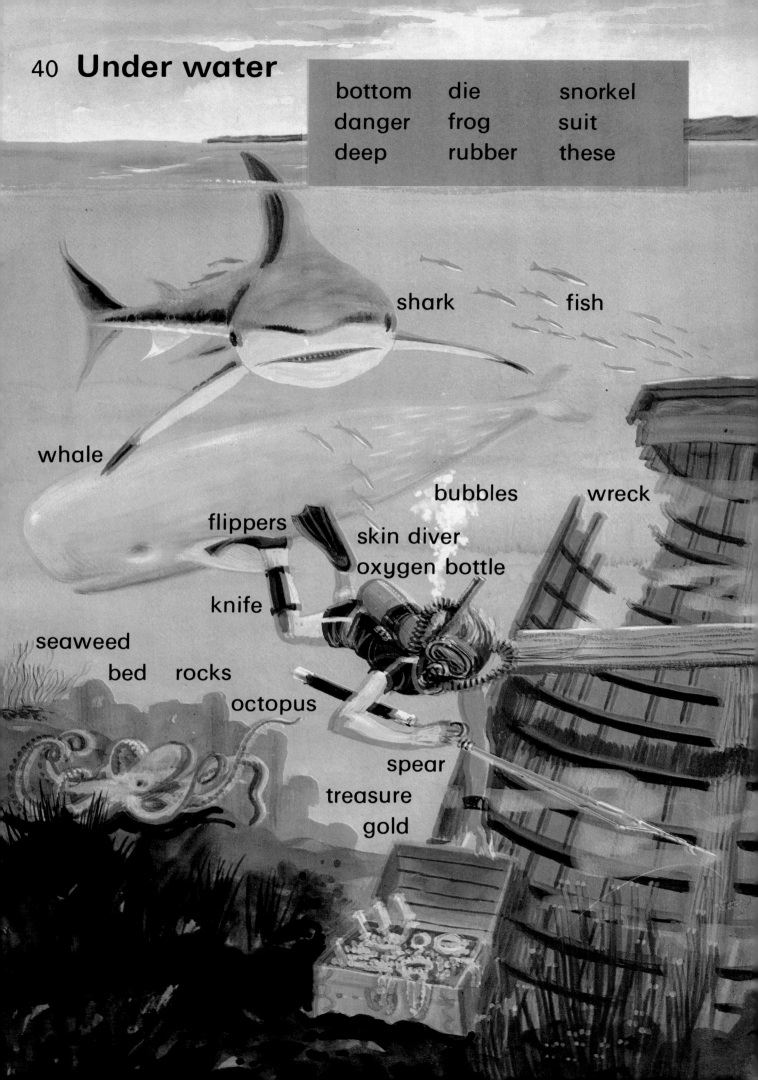

bottom   die   snorkel
danger   frog   suit
deep   rubber   these

shark

fish

whale

bubbles

wreck

flippers

skin diver

oxygen bottle

knife

seaweed

bed   rocks

octopus

spear

treasure

gold

dead
dig
dirty
grass
ground
grow
picnic
pot
use

line

trees

packet seeds

swing

arch

rustic

hedge

flower-bed

pool

seat

lawn

mower

roller

fork

spade

rake

hoe

watering-can

wheelbarrow

path

hose

trowel

42 When I grow up

babies   sell   you
house   teacher   your
old   told
race   try

driver

farmer

doctor

fireman

nurse

builder

astronaut

policeman

footballer

pilot   air hostess

shopkeeper

model

kennel-maid

A caravan holiday 43

awning food level
eat gas pull
entrance hill tidy
fasten hurry toilet

roof ladder bunk beds

seats sleep curtain

view tents

...cking
busy
ready
cases

site

shop rows

front back
door

rest step

...ive towing excited

windows

bar wheel

SEAVIEW
CARAVAN SITE

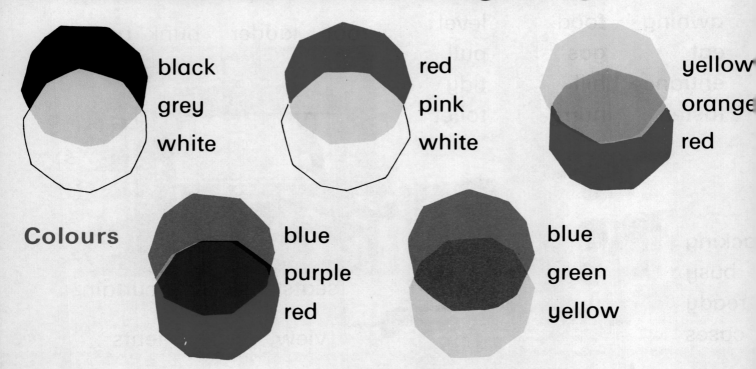

black
grey
white

red
pink
white

yellow
orange
red

Colours

blue
purple
red

blue
green
yellow

Numbers

1	one
2	two
3	three
4	four
5	five
6	six
7	seven
8	eight
9	nine
10	ten
20	twenty
30	thirty
40	forty
50	fifty
100	one hundred

Beginnings

Once upon a time . . .
Not long ago . . .
This morning . . .
I always remember . . .
Yesterday . . .
Have you ever been . . .?
Last year . . .
Daddy was ever so pleased when . . .
I have always wanted . . .
My Mummy says . . .
I always like going . . .
My favourite pet is . . .
Every night . . .
At week-ends I . . .
When I am in the town . . .
In our garden . . .
At school we often . . .
I am going to be . . .
It is very exciting to . . .
I must tell you about . . .

word	page
seal	17
seals	12
search	15
seaside	32
seat	17,35,41
seats	43
seaweed	32,40
secret	9
seeds	22,41
seek	16
sell	20,42
send	39
set	11
seven	44
shark	40
shed	21
sheep	21
sheets	28
shelf	5
shells	32
shelves	20
shepherds	13
sheriff	24
shining	10
ships	33
shirt	1,24,32
shoes	20
shoot	24
shop	43
shopkeeper	42
shopping	20
shops	26
short	2,3
shorts	1,32
show	11,38
shows	3
side	4,25
sign	24
signal	29,35
signs	25
silver	20
sing	19,23,31
singing	13
sink	5,28
sister	6
sit	11,14,19
site	43
six	23,44
skin	36,40
skins	24
skip	16
skirt	2
sky	22
sledging	30
sleep	37,43
sleet	30
sleeve	1
slide	16
sliding	30
slipper	9
smart	2

word	page
smiling	8
smoke	10
snorkel	40
snow	13,30
snowball	30
snowdrop	27
snowman	30
so	44
socks	1
soft	7
softly	30
soldier	8
something	28
sometimes	34
soon	10
soup	18
sour	36
sou'wester	30
space	39
spaceman	8
spade	32,41
sparkler	10
sparrow	31
spear	40
spray	34
spurs	24
square	26
stable	7,21
stage	19
stairs	5,28
stamp	38
stand	19
star	9,13
starfish	32
starling	31
start	10
station	26,35,39
statue	26
stay	32,37
steamer	33
step	4,43
stetson	8,24
sticks	10
still	30
stilts	17
stockings	1
stone	9
stones	36
stony	24
stop	15,35
storm	30
story	14,19
straight	1
straw	21,37
strawberries	36
streamer	13
street	4,25
stroke	7
suit	3,8,39,40
sum	14

word	page
sun	30,32
sunny	30
sunshine	30
supermarket	26
swan	31
sweater	1
sweep	28
sweet	18,36
sweets	20
swim	32
swing	16,41
switch	11
sword	8

t

word	page
tabby	7
table	5,23,28
tail	17,31
take	29,34,38
take-off	29
takes	2
tall	2,3
talons	31
tame	12
tan	30
tanker	29
taps	5
tarts	18
taste	36
taxi	35
tea	18,19,23
teacher	14,19,42
telephone	37
television	11
tell	14,44
temperature	37
ten	44
tent	17
tents	43
thanks	19
the	12,30,44
thermometer	37
these	40
thick	30
think	29
thirty	44
this	44
three	44
through	5
throw	16
thrush	31
thunder	30
ticket	17
tidy	43
tiger	12
tiles	5
time	23,44
tins	20

word	page
tiny	31
to	37,44
toast	18
today	17
together	6
toilet	5,43
told	42
tomahawk	24
tomatoes	19
tomorrow	17
tonight	11
took	12
top	17
towel	32
tower	17
towing	43
town	25,26,44
toys	16
track	35
tractor	21
traffic	15,25
trapeze	17
treasure	9,40
tree	4,13
trees	41
tricks	9
tricycle	16
trip	29,33
trolley	20
trousers	1,3
trowel	41
truck	35
trunks	32
try	20,42
T shirt	32
tulip	27
tune	19
turn	16,29
turtle	12
T V	4,11
twenty	44
two	44
tyre	10

u

word	page
umbrella	8,30
uncle	6
under	5,27,40
uniform	8,15
until	37
up	8,42
upon	44
use	41

50

	page
V	
van	25,35,38
vanish	9
vase	27
vegetables	18,19
very	23,32,44
view	29,43
visit	26,32
vulture	31

W	
wagging	7
waistcoat	24
wait	35
waiting	32
wake	37
walk	34,39
wall	4
wallflower	27
wand	9
wanted	44
wardrobe	5
warm	30
warship	33
was	44
wash	34
washer	5
wash up	28
wasp	22
watch	3,11
watching	11
water	14,18, 32,40
watering-can	41
wave	15
waves	33
we	16,44
wear	8
weather	30
webbed	31
wedding	6
week	11,44
week-ends	44
weigh	20
welcome	23
well	9
wellingtons	30
Wendy	14
Western	11
wet	28,30
whale	40
wheel	10,16,34
wheelbarrow	41
when	42,44
where	4
white	30,31,44
wigwam	24

	page
wild	12
wind	22,30
window	4
windows	43
windy	30
wings	31
winter	31
wireless	15
wishing	9
witch	9
wizard	9
wobbling	25
wolf	12
woman	2
won	13
wood	10
woodpecker	31
woods	21
wool	21
work	3
works	2
would	15
wreck	40
wren	31
write	14,23,38

y	
yacht	33
yard	21
year	44
yellow	44
yes	23
yesterday	28,44
you	23,42,44
your	42

z	
zebra	12
zip	29
zoo	12

BATH COLLEGE
OF
HIGHER EDUCATION
NEWTON PARK
LIBRARY

CLASS No. J423 SIM o/s

ACC No. 837875

SW

037698